The C.E.O.'s
Little Instruction Book

Presented By

Van Crouch Communications

Trade Life Books
Tulsa, Oklahoma

D1545625

The C.E.O.'s Little Instruction Book
ISBN 1-57757-039-1
Copyright © 1999 by Trade Life Books
P. O. Box 55325
Tulsa, Oklahoma 74155

Presented by *Van Crouch Communications*
P. O. Box 320
Wheaton, Illinois 60189

Introduction

They're men and women of influence and persuasion. You rarely know what they're thinking. But you wish you did! You infrequently get an audience with them. But you wish you could!

They're called "Big-wigs," "Moneymakers," "Controversial," "Successful"; yet, they're ordinary human beings like you and me who decided to risk the extraordinary—and prevailed.

Now, with *The C.E.O.'s Little Instruction Book,* you have access to the inner chamber of these exceptional executive minds! Packed into this little pocketbook are the creativity, genius, inspiration, and talent that have taken these successful men and women from the cubicle to the corner office.

Learn of their passions and purposes—their fervor to live lives set apart, to rise above the daily struggles with resilience, to make a distinctive difference.

The road to success is always under construction.

John W. Patten
Former Publisher
***Business Week* Magazine**

[Patten's career with book publisher McGraw-Hill led him to his role as publisher of *Business Week*. Under his guidance, the magazine expanded its readership to more than one million, launched three foreign-language editions, and won the industry's highest honor.]

5

One who never asks either knows everything or nothing.

Malcolm Forbes Sr.

Former Chairman
***Forbes* Magazine**

[Forbes inherited *Forbes Magazine* from his father and built it into a successful business with more than half a million subscribers.]

T*o me, it's very simple;
if you're going to be thinking anyway,
you might as well think big.*

Donald Trump

Chairman
Trump Organization

[Billionaire Trump started in business as a developer in New York City.]

Nothing in the world can take
the place of persistence. . . .

The quality of an individual is reflected
in the standards they set for themselves.

Ray Kroc
Former Chairman
McDonald's

[Kroc built his organization with an emphasis on automation and standardization of operations. Today, McDonald's is the international icon of the fast food industry.]

*The world stands on its head . . .
for those few and far between souls
who devote 100 percent.*

Andrew Carnegie
Founder
Carnegie Steel Company

[Carnegie worked for a cotton factory, a telegraph office, and the Pennsylvania Railroad. He founded several steel mills, eventually consolidating his vast holdings into the Carnegie Steel Company.]

*Success is a journey,
not a destination.*

Joseph Gorman
Chairman
TRW, Inc.

[Gorman joined the auto industry after his graduation from Yale. TRW is currently one of the major auto parts suppliers to Detroit's Big Three.]

G*reat achievement is usually born of great sacrifice and is never the result of selfishness.*

Napoleon Hill
Founder
Napoleon Hill Associates

[Andrew Carnegie gave Hill a unique, lengthy assignment: research and interview the nation's most successful men. The assignment became Hill's first published work, which later evolved into his well-known book, *Think and Grow Rich.*]

Nothing can be accomplished
until you begin.

*Success is much more quickly
attained when you expect it.*

Ira Hayes

Manager
Advertising Department
NCR Corporation

[Hayes is the organizer of the Speakers' Bureau, and he is widely recognized as the "Ambassador of Enthusiasm" for his authority on positive thinking and motivational behavior.]

G*enius is 1 percent inspiration and 99 percent perspiration.*

Thomas A. Edison

Inventor and Founder
Edison Electric Light Company

[Although he is known for many inventions, one of Edison's greatest contributions was founding Edison Electric Light Company to generate, transmit, and distribute electric power.]

All *of life is the management of risk, not its elimination.*

Walter Wriston
Former Chairman
Citicorp

[After joining Citibank in 1946, Wriston worked his way up the corporate ladder, becoming president and C.E.O. in 1967. He was named chairman of Citicorp in 1970. Wriston also serves on the boards of several other companies.]

Never get discouraged and never quit
because if you never quit,
you're never beaten.

Ted Turner
Founder
Turner Broadcasting System

[Turner used his billboard business to buy a failing Atlanta television station, which he turned into a great success. He subsequently bought the Atlanta Braves, launched CNN, and acquired MGM.]

M*ost people get ahead during*
the time that others waste.

Failure is only the opportunity to
begin again more intelligently.

Henry Ford
Founder
Ford Motor Company

[Ford disliked life on the farm near Dearborn, Michigan, where he was born. But his love and aptitude for machinery resulted in the development of the first mass-produced car in the world, the Model T, and the founding of the Ford Motor Company.]

You are the same today that you are going to be five years from now except for two things: the people . . . you associate with, and the books you read.

Charles "Tremendous" Jones

President
Life Management Services, Inc.

[Jones' company helps to empower corporate management in seminars held throughout the United States. He is also a renowned writer and speaker.]

You *can't run a business*
without taking risks.

Millard Drexler

C.E.O.
The Gap

[Since joining The Gap in 1983, Drexler has widened its appeal with new outlets like Gap Kids and Old Navy, helping to transform the company into a premier specialty retailer.]

N*o sale is really complete until the product is worn out and the customer is satisfied.*

Leon Leonwood Bean

Founder
L. L. Bean, Inc.

[In 1912, Bean, an avid outdoorsman, concocted a hybrid hunting boot. He sold them by mail, promising full refunds if customers weren't satisfied. Ninety of his first hundred pairs fell apart yet he fulfilled his guarantee as he perfected his product. Meeting such a standard enables L. L. Bean, Inc. to thrive today.]

Winners *are just ex-losers who got mad.*

You're not finished when you're defeated . . .
you're finished when you quit.

William V. Crouch

President
Van Crouch Communications, Inc.

[After ranking as a consistent sales leader with the American Express Company and receiving awards for outstanding performance in the insurance industry, Crouch qualified as a member of the Million Dollar Round Table. He is one of America's most versatile speakers.]

A *man who trims himself to suit everybody will soon whittle himself away.*

Charles Schwab

Former President
Bethlehem Steel

[Schwab started working in Andrew Carnegie's steel mills and worked his way through various management positions until he was named president of Carnegie Steel. He bought Bethlehem Steel Company from Carnegie and expanded the business during World War I.]

$$\text{Do not fear mistakes.}$$
Wisdom is often born of . . . mistakes.

Paul Galvin
Founder
Motorola

[In the 1930s, Galvin founded Motorola to mass-produce car radios. His company has created such products as cellular phones, pagers, and semiconductors.]

The urge to quit is the last obstacle
between you and your dreams.

Richard DeVos

Cofounder and Former President
Amway Corporation

[DeVos cofounded one of the world's largest privately held companies.
The recently retired president is an acclaimed author and speaker.]

Intellect doesn't determine success —
good choices do.

*Motivation comes from that
which we value most.*

Jim Cathcart
Former President
National Speakers' Association

[Cathcart, founder of a consulting firm in La Jolla, California, is also a partner in a psychological research firm in Carefree, Arizona.]

T*he only place success comes before work is in the dictionary.*

Donald Kendall

Former Chairman
PepsiCo

[Although technically retired from the company, Kendall still devotes time to expanding PepsiCo's international fast food market. He also chairs an international investment fund, runs two cattle ranches, and heads the National Forest Foundation conservation group.]

25

The only pretty store is
the one full of people.

William T. Dillard

Founder
Dillard's Department Stores

[Dillard began his retailing chain with a single store in Nashville, Arkansas. Dillard's pioneered the use of electronic cash registers and computerized systems and generates annual sales of several billion dollars.]

M*y only business secret [is] . . .*
to work harder than everybody else.

H. Wayne Huizenga
Owner
Miami Dolphins

[Billionaire Huizenga—"the man with the golden touch"—raised the worth of Atlanta-based Waste Management from $5 million upon acquisition to $3 billion. His second purchase, Blockbuster, grew from a market value of $32 million to $8.4 billion at the time he sold it in 1994.]

The time to be toughest is
when things are going the best.

Donald Keough
Former President
Coca-Cola

[Keough was president of Coca-Cola upon his retirement in 1993. He serves on the boards of the H. J. Heinz Company, National Service Industries, and the *Washington Post*.]

Self-confidence is important.
Confidence in others is essential.

William A. Schreyer

Former C.E.O.
Merrill Lynch & Co., Inc.

[Under Schreyer's leadership, Merrill Lynch revenues skyrocketed, and its stock price quadrupled in the early 1990s.]

Motivation will always beat mere talent.

Norman R. Augustine
C.E.O.
Martin Marietta Corp.

[Prior to joining Martin Marietta, Augustine held positions at the assistant and undersecretary level in the Defense Department. He serves as a member of the boards of Phillips Petroleum, Riggs National Corp., and Procter and Gamble.]

*If you put fences around people,
you get sheep.*

Livio DeSimone

C.E.O.
3M

[DeSimone went to work for 3M right out of college. He worked his way through the ranks to become C.E.O.]

Exceed your customers' expectations. . . .
Give them what they want – and a little more.

There is only one boss: the customer. And he can fire everybody in the company, from the chairman on down, simply by spending his money somewhere else.

Sam Walton
Founder
Wal-Mart Stores

[The legendary Walton learned how to deliver customer satisfaction early in his career as a retailer. He went on to build a five-and-dime store into the world's largest retail company.]

K*eep an open attitude and be willing to try new things.*

Arthur C. Martinez

C.E.O.
Sears Roebuck

[Martinez is credited with guiding a major overhaul of Sears in the early 1990s. In his first year of leadership, the retailer earned more than $1 billion after losing $3.9 billion the year before.]

D*on't sit down and wait for opportunities to come. . . . Get up and make them!*

Madam C. J. Walker

Founder
Madam C. J. Walker Manufacturing Company

[Walker, born "Sarah Breedlove," the daughter of former slaves, was married at 14 and widowed at 20. She invented a hair care product that took the industry by storm, and by 1917 she was considered New York's wealthiest black woman.]

W_{ith} *[creativity] most challenges can be met. Without it, problems are seldom converted into opportunities.*

David Fagin
Chairman
Golden Star Resources, Ltd.

[When American Goldfields, Inc. and Golden Star Resources, Ltd. merged in 1992, the new company needed an able leader—experienced and reputable. They found the leadership they needed in Fagin, then president of Homestake Mining Co.]

Success is achieved through making a decision, making it yours, and dying by it.

Don't spend your life trying to make right decisions; invest your life making decisions and making them right.

Charles "Tremendous" Jones

President
Life management Services, Inc.

[In addition to his work as a renowned writer and speaker, Jones oversees a company that helps to empower corporate management in seminars held throughout the United States.]

Success comes from a constant focus on renewal.

Gary Tooker
C.E.O.
Motorola

[Tooker joined Motorola in 1962 in the semiconductor section of the company. He steadily worked his way up to become chief executive officer.]

The most important thing in the Olympic games is not winning but taking part . . . The essential thing in life is not conquering but fighting well.

Baron Pierre de Coubertin

Founder & First President
International Olympic Committee

[In 1894, de Coubertin set out to re-create the ancient Greek Olympics as a means of promoting international fellowship and sports proficiency. The Olympic Games remain an international event that draws thousands of athletes from all over the world.]

Leaders get results through people.

Patricia Fripp
Former President
National Speakers' Association

[Fripp began as a hairstylist at age 15 in England. She moved to San Francisco with only $500 in her pocket and began building her clientele. Three years later, she was one of the first women working in the men's hairstyling profession and today operates a very successful salon and product distribution business.]

*Success does not come to you.
You go to it.*

If it is to be, it is up to me.

Wally Amos
Founder
Famous Amos

[Amos left Florida at age 12 to live with an aunt in New York. After she introduced him to homemade chocolate chip cookies, he traded plans for a career in entertainment for a cookie business that is thriving today.]

The customer is the boss.

David Glass
C.E.O.
Wal-Mart

[Glass has engineered many innovations that have kept Wal-Mart at the forefront of the retailing industry. His strategies include placing discount stores and Sam's Club warehouses side by side to exploit their marketing synergies.]

Hire *people who are more talented than [you] are.*

Steven Leebow

Founder and C.E.O.
Pacesetter Steel

[Leebow founded Pacesetter Steel in 1977. Since 1983, the Fortune 500 company has made in excess of $100 million dollars in sales. One of Pacesetter's competitors is Majestic Steel Service—a company founded by Steven's younger brother, Dennis.]

42

I*t is only as we develop others that we permanently succeed.*

Harvey S. Firestone

Founder
Firestone Tire & Rubber Company

[Firestone formed the Firestone Tire & Rubber Company in 1900 and served as president until 1932. He was the first supplier of tires to Ford Motor Company and became a major national supplier by the 1930s.]

Honesty *is the cornerstone of all success.*

Recognition is the most powerful of all motivators. Even criticism can build confidence when it's "sandwiched" between layers of praise.

Mary Kay Ash
Founder
Mary Kay Cosmetics

[Ash started her cosmetics company with her son Richard, who is now chairman of the million-dollar firm. The company's phenomenal success is credited to her ability to motivate her sales force to market her products. She remains active in the company as chairman emeritus.]

D*on't lose sleep over problems*
that may go away.

Richard Jenrette

Cofounder
Donaldson, Lufkin, & Jenrette

[Jenrette cofounded his Wall Street company during a recession that put most rival firms out of business. Under his leadership, DLJ survived, and Jenrette remained C.E.O. until it was bought by Equitable in 1985.]

The will to persevere is
often the difference between
failure and success.

David Sarnoff
Founder
NBC

[Sarnoff pioneered development of the first commercial radio set in 1916, which became very popular after an audience of more than 300,000 tuned in to his broadcast of the Dempsey-Carpentier boxing match. In time, he became president of RCA, set up the first experimental television station, and founded NBC.]

There's no telling how far
a person can go if he's willing
to let other people take the credit.

Robert Woodruff

Former C.E.O.
Coca-Cola

[After Ernest Woodruff bought Coca-Cola, he hired his son Robert to run it. Robert made Coca-Cola into an international household name.]

Leadership is practiced not so much in words as in attitude and in actions.

What you manage in business is people.

Harold Geneen
C.E.O.
ITT

[Geneen forged his reputation as an effective, tough-minded accountant at Jones & Laughlin, Bell & Howell, and at Raytheon before taking over ITT. Throughout the 1960s and '70s, he masterminded ITT's tremendous growth from a company grossing less than $800 million annually to $22 billion.]

P*roductivity is the name of the game.*

William Hewlett

Cofounder
Hewlett Packard

[Hewlett and Dave Packard credit much of their drive and inspiration to a Stanford college professor, whose support inspired them to begin Hewlett Packard in Packard's garage. Their first major customer: the Walt Disney Company.]

W*hen you're building mountains,
it's best not to look at those
God has already made.*

Ron Toomer

President
Arrow Dynamics

[When Arrow Dynamics reentered the roller-coaster business, it chose Toomer as its first engineer. Under his leadership, Arrow Dynamics is today the principal roller-coaster builder in the world.]

*Consumers are statistics.
Customers are people.*

Stanley Marcus
Chairman Emeritus
Neiman-Marcus

[Taking over a business founded by his father, uncle, and aunt in 1907, Marcus made Neiman-Marcus a successful business synonymous with tasteful, upscale shopping.]

F*ear of failure must never be a reason not to try something.*

Leadership is both something you are and something you do.

Frederick Smith

Founder
Federal Express

[Smith's success didn't come overnight. But in 1983, Federal Express became the company that reached a billion dollars in revenue in the shortest length of time.]

T*he real secret of success is enthusiasm. Yes, more than enthusiasm, I say excitement. I like to see men get excited. When they get excited they make a success of their lives.*

Walter P. Chrysler

Founder
Chrysler Corporation

[Beginning his automotive career as a machinist, Chrysler quickly rose through the ranks to become president of Buick Motor Company, a division of General Motors, in 1916. Five years later, he joined the Maxwell Motor Company, which in 1925 became Chrysler Corporation.]

D*o common things
uncommonly well.*

Henry J. Heinz
Cofounder and President
H. J. Heinz & Co.

[Heinz was a producer of prepared foods who, with his brother and
cousin, founded a partnership that became the H. J. Heinz Company.
Heinz was named president when it was incorporated in 1905.]

A*ccomplishment influences confidence, and confidence influences accomplishment.*

Harold S. Hook

Chairman
American General Corp.

[Hook went to work for American General as president of a subsidiary. In 1975, he was elected corporation president and subsequently took over as chairman and C.E.O. He retired in 1996.]

Eagles don't flock—you have
to find them one at a time.

Any company that spends a lot of time on internal
fighting will lose the battle against the competition.

H. Ross Perot

Founder
Electronic Data Systems

[While Perot was working at IBM, he founded Electronic Data Systems. By the time he sold it to General Motors in 1984, it was worth more than $2 billion. Four years later, Perot returned to the computer industry and formed the Perot Systems Corporation.]

P*rocrastination is opportunity's natural assassin.*

Victor Kiam

Former Chairman
Remington Products, Inc.

[Kiam worked for International Latex Corporation and then owned Benrus Watch Company, Inc. before he bought Remington Products.]

Credentials are not the same as accomplishments.

Robert Half

President
Robert Half International

[Half is founder and president of a highly successful recruiting firm with offices on three continents. He is author of the bestseller, *The Robert Half Way to Get Hired in Today's Job Market.*]

Perceptions may count in the short term, but substance always prevails.

Barbara Capsalis
Senior Vice President
Chemical Bank of New York

[When she graduated from college, Capsalis planned to work one to two years, get married, and live happily ever after. Years later, she is still married—and still working. She is responsible for Chemical's non-credit services worldwide and manages 2,500 people.]

A *leader is . . . someone who carries water for his people so that they can get on with their jobs.*

If you don't do it excellently, don't do it at all.

Robert Townsend
Former President
Avis

[Townsend, a former director of American Express, engineered a major turnaround that brought Avis into the black for the first time in 13 years. Currently, he is an author and renowned speaker.]

Problems are only opportunities
in work clothes.

Henry J. Kaiser
Founder
Kaiser Industries

[Kaiser opened his health care business when he realized that the close of
World War II spelled the end for shipbuilding operations. As of 1990,
Kaiser Industries had 6.5 million members in 16 states.]

N*ever think a job is more than you can do.*
Your potential is unlimited if you
just put your mind to it.

Patricia Lindh
Vice President, Wholesale Marketing
Bank of America

[Seven years after she retired and married, Lindh was appointed liaison with women's organizations during the Nixon administration. She served as special assistant for women and later deputy assistant secretary of state for educational and cultural affairs in the Ford administration.]

An *environment of uncertainty produces a lot of fear.*

Robert Haas

C.E.O.
Levi Strauss & Company

[Haas is the great-great-grandnephew of Levi Strauss, founder of the company. He has maintained the company's position as the world's largest apparel maker.]

E*xperience, if it doesn't kill you, teaches you how to bounce back.*

Success is not so much achievement as achieving.

David J. Mahoney
Founder
Banyan Systems Inc.

[Mahoney formed Banyan Systems in 1983 to provide network operating systems to businesses. Today, Banyan Systems commands almost half of the U. S. market.]

There may be luck in getting a job,
but there's no luck in keeping it.

J. Ogden Armour
Former President
Armour Meat Packing Company

[After he inherited his father's meat packing company, Armour built it into
the world's largest.]

M*y formula for success?*
Rise early, work late, strike oil.

Jean Paul Getty
Founder
Getty Oil Co.

[Getty made his first million at the age of 23 in the Oklahoma oil business. He founded Getty Oil Company and was considered the richest man in the world by 1957.]

You *have to believe*
in the impossible.

Howard Head

Founder
Head Skis
Prince Tennis

[Head revolutionized two sports industries simply because he wanted to improve his own abilities. His inventions proved so successful that Head Skis and Prince Tennis products are considered the status symbols of their respective sports.]

The key to successful leadership . . .
is influence, not authority.

Serve your people and help them win.

Kenneth H. Blanchard

Cofounder and Chairman
Blanchard Training & Development

[A sought-after speaker and business consultant, Blanchard has written several books on management, including the best-selling *One Minute Manager.* He also holds a faculty position in leadership at the University of Massachusetts and a visiting lectureship at Cornell University.]

W*ork is the basis of living. . . .
A man will rust out quicker
than he'll wear out.*

Colonel Harland Sanders

Founder
Kentucky Fried Chicken

[At an age when most people retire, 65-year-old Sanders began selling his secret recipe for fried chicken. And with that recipe, he built a multimillion-dollar food franchise.]

It is well to think well;
it is divine to act well.

Horace Mann
President
Antioch College

[Mann practiced law in Massachusetts before being elected a state senator. He kept his seat until he was appointed secretary to the Board of Education in 1837. Through his efforts, the public school system enjoyed dramatic improvements.]

Unless you're going to be a violinist or something, your success will . . . depend on other people.

William G. McGowan

Founder and Former Chairman
MCI Communications Corp.

[Through tireless lobbying efforts, McGowan, founder of MCI, sparked a series of FCC regulatory decisions, including the landmark grant to MCI to offer competitive services. MCI is currently one of the largest long distance corporations in the world.]

I*f you can dream it, you can do it.*
Remember, this whole thing was
started by a mouse.

Without inspiration . . . we would perish.

Walt Disney
Founder
Walt Disney Corporation

[Disney launched his dream out of a Hollywood garage by perfecting cartoons. His success led to the creation of the world's first animated film, "Snow White and the Seven Dwarfs."]

Money is a very excellent servant but a terrible master.

P. T. Barnum
Cofounder
Barnum & Bailey's Circus

[Barnum developed a New York City museum into a popular attraction and combined the many elements into a huge circus, "The Greatest Show on Earth." Ten years later, he and his chief rival joined forces to become "The Barnum & Bailey's Circus."]

G*roundless hope, like unconditional love, is the only kind worth having.*

John Perry Barlow
Vice Chairman
Electronic Frontier Foundation

[Barlow left the cattle business to cofound Electronic Frontier Foundation (EFF) with Mitchell Kapor, former C.E.O. of Lotus Development Corp. EFF is the leading public-interest group focusing on civil liberties in electronic communications.]

The new source of power is not money in the hands of a few but information in the hands of many.

John Naisbitt

Chairman
Naisbitt Group

[Naisbitt is a social forecaster, speaker, and advisor to America's leading companies, such as AT&T, United Technologies, IBM, General Electric, and Control Data. An entrepreneur since 1968, he has worked for IBM, Eastman Kodak, and the White House.]

There is no substitute for hard work.

Good fortune is what happens when opportunity meets with preparation.

Thomas A. Edison

Inventor and Founder
Edison Electric Light Company

[Known for many inventions, Edison's greatest contribution may be the first electric power generating station. Its success led to the founding of Edison Electric Light Company, which later merged into the General Electric Company.]

Goodwill is the one and
only asset that competition
cannot undersell or destroy.

Marshall Field
Founder
Marshall Field & Co.

[Beginning in 1865, Field built Marshall Field & Co. into a million-dollar retail business and expanded into manufacturing and wholesale markets. In the early 1900s, Field Enterprises founded the *Chicago Sun* (later merged with the *Sun-Times*), and published the *World Book Encyclopedia*.]

Think diversity.
The idea of trying
everything is important.

Jill Elikann Barad

President
Mattel, Inc.

[Barad decided against becoming a doctor when she fainted during her first time in an operating room. She tried acting, cosmetics, and advertising before she became product manager at Mattel in 1981 and engineered Barbie's maturation into a versatile career woman.]

Management's job is to see
the company not as it is . . .
but as it can become.

John W. Teets
C.E.O.
Dial Corporation

[When he assumed Dial's leadership, Teets completely overhauled the failing company. Through his efforts, Dial Corporation turned profitable, and its stock price doubled.]

If *you want to succeed in business,*
liberate other people's gifts.

The only thing that stands between a man and
what he wants from life is . . . the will to
try it and the faith to believe. . . .

Richard DeVos

Cofounder and Former President
Amway Corporation

[DeVos recently retired as president of one of the largest privately held companies in the world. He is an acclaimed author and speaker.]

The commitment to using the very best in all of us . . . is the umbrella over quality, customer satisfaction, profitability, efficiency—everything.

Alex Troutman

C.E.O.
Ford Motor Company

[Four years after his Royal Air Force discharge, Troutman joined Ford-Britain. He quickly moved up in rank, eventually becoming president and chairman of Ford of Europe. In 1993, Troutman took over as chairman of Ford Motor Company.]

During my eighty-seven years, I have witnessed
a whole succession of technological revolutions.
But none of them has done away with the need for
character in the individual or the ability to think.

Bernard M. Baruch

Chairman
War Industries Board of World War I

[Baruch enjoyed a prosperous career at a Wall Street brokerage house.
During World War I, he chaired the War Industries Board and was a
delegate and economic advisor at the Paris Peace Conference. He later
served as an economic advisor to the U.S. government.]

G*reat successes are built on taking . . .*
a negative and turning it into a positive—
overcoming hazard, overcoming danger,
overcoming catastrophe.

Sumner Redstone

Chairman
Viacom

[At age 63, Redstone, owner of a highly successful theater chain, began buying stock in a small cable company and set out to learn what he could about the business. Today, Redstone is a major conglomerate and owner of Viacom, a multi-billion dollar company.]

Until you risk everything . . .
you're never going to lead.

Constructive criticism is never identified by the
mouth speaking but by the ears listening.

Dr. Tom Haggai
Chairman
Independent Grocers Alliance (IGA)

[Haggai hosts a daily radio show, "One Minute, Please." Despite his busy schedule, he finds time to give major national and international addresses nearly every week.]

T*he only way you can measure*
character is by reputation.

Roberto Goizueta

C.E.O.
Coca-Cola

[Goizueta began working for Coca-Cola as a chemist in his native Cuba. Through hard work and dedication, he advanced quickly through the ranks until he was named chairman in 1981.]

Satisfied employees are a necessary precondition for satisfied customers.

Ira Stepanian
Former C.E.O.
Bank of Boston

[Stepanian began his career as a management trainee, rising steadily to higher-level positions until he was named president in 1983. He saved the Bank of Boston from financial disaster caused by a mountain of bad loans.]

[H*ire*] *outstanding people. . . .*
If [there is] a secret weapon, this is it.

James Henderson
C.E.O.
Cummins Engine

[A former faculty member at Harvard Business School, Henderson started at Cummins as an assistant to the chairman. He was named chairman in 1995. Currently, he is a trustee at Princeton and is president of the trustees for Culver Educational Foundation.]

A *problem well stated is
a problem half solved.*

Believe and act as if it were impossible to fail.

Charles F. Kettering

Cofounder
Sloan-Kettering Institute for Cancer Research

[In 1908, Kettering improved the ignition system that revolutionized the auto industry. Four years later, the Cadillac Division of General Motors turned to Kettering's new company for components that combined ignition, lighting, and the first electric self-starter.]

Do what you set out to do.

John K. Hanson
Founder
Winnebago Industries, Inc.

[In the late 1950s, Hanson led a group that persuaded Modernistic Industries to build a travel trailer manufacturing plant in Forest City, Iowa. In 1959, he took over the plant. When he took Winnebago public, in 1971, its stock rose 462%.]

Develop *a product where*
there is no market—
then create one.

Akio Morita

Cofounder
Sony

[Although Morita's background is in engineering, he is credited with Sony's worldwide sales and marketing success. He "engineered" Sony's purchase of CBS Records and Columbia Pictures, making the company a dominant force in the entertainment industry.]

A *career adventure is the
better way to think about life.*

Roger Enrico
C.E.O.
PepsiCo

[Enrico began at PepsiCo in 1971 as an associate production manager in the Frito-Lay Division. He worked his way up to become president of PepsiCo Foods Japan and president of PepsiCo, and then PepsiCo C.E.O. in 1996.]

Wen the product is right, you don't have to be a great marketer.

You can have brilliant ideas, but if you can't get them across, your ideas won't get you anywhere.

Lee Iacocca
Former Chairman
Chrysler Corporation

[Iacocca began his automotive career at Ford, moving up the corporate ladder to eventually become president. After being fired, he joined the failing Chrysler Corporation where his strategies turned it into a profoundly lucrative business.]

The great pleasure in life is doing what people say you cannot do.

Walter Bagehot
Former Editor
The Economist

[Bagehot introduced the treasury bill, the bank rate, and the notion of a central bank taking responsibility for the value of a nation's currency. His enduring classic, *The English Constitution,* written in 1867, remains an insightful account of the inner workings of the British political system.]

Time *is the friend of
the wonderful company,
the enemy of the mediocre.*

Warren Buffett
C.E.O.
Berkshire Hathaway, Inc.

[Buffet began as an investment salesman for his father's brokerage firm.
At age 25, he formed Buffett-Partnership, a limited partnership investment
fund. In 1969, he took over Berkshire Hathaway, a small textile company
with current holdings in excess of $2 billion.]

D*on't hold the penny so close to your eye that you can't see the dollar behind it.*

Mike Markkula
Cofounder and Chairman
Apple Computer

[A former marketing executive at Intel, Markkula helped launch Apple Computer by providing financing and supervision to Apple cofounders, Steve Wozniak and Steven Jobs.]

Success or failure [of a business] depends on the attitudes of the employees.

Donald Keough
Former President
Coca-Cola

[Keough was president of Coca-Cola until his retirement in 1993. He is a board member of the H. J. Heinz Company, National Service Industries, and the *Washington Post.*]

L*ife is about how you deal with adversity.*

Diana "Dede" Brooks

C.E.O.
Sotheby's

[When Brooks began with Sotheby's, she immediately caught the attention of owner Alfred Taubman. Under her leadership, Sotheby's has become a widely respected auction house.]

Winning organizations will be those that give individuals the chance to personally make a difference.

John Sculley

Former C.E.O.
Apple Computer Co.

[Sculley was a Pepsi marketer when Apple hired him as C.E.O. He left Apple for Spectrum Technologies until Kodak retained him as an advisor to help build its digital imaging and brand marketing strategies.]

The battle belongs to the persistent.
Refuse to let friends or
circumstances defeat you.

William V. Crouch

President
Van Crouch Communications, Inc.

[A consistent sales leader with American Express, Crouch won many
awards for outstanding performance in the insurance industry and
became a member of the Million Dollar Round Table. He is the author of
several bestsellers and one of America's most versatile speakers.]

Ineffective leaders often act on the advice and counsel of the last person they talked to.

Leadership is the capacity to translate vision into reality.

Warren G. Bennis

Former President
University of Cincinnati

[Bennis, a distinguished professor of business administration at the University of Southern California, has served as president of the University of Cincinnati and chairman of Organizational Studies at the Massachusetts Institute of Technology's Sloan School of Management.]

W*hen [people] work in a place that cares about them, they contribute a lot more than "duty."*

Dennis Hayes

C.E.O.
Hayes Microcomputer Products, Inc.

[Hayes founded one of the fastest growing companies in the United States. As a member of the Georgia Governor's Advisory Council on Science and Technology, he keeps the governor and legislature abreast of technology and science issues.]

Ethics must begin at the top of an organization.

Edward L. Hennessy Jr.

Former C.E.O.
Allied Signal, Inc.

[Edward was Allied's C.E.O. for two decades until his retirement in 1991.]

D*evelop confidence in yourself*
and act as if you have it until you do.

Barbara Krouse

Vice President
Product Development
Stouffer Foods Corporation

[Krouse began with Stouffer's as a research assistant, rising to assistant manager of research & development and then manager. Her research into tasty, non-fattening, easy-to-fix dinners became the basis for Stouffer's successful Lean Cuisine products.]

Dismiss *personal grudges promptly.*

Tact is the personal ingredient that smoothes out the rough spots of life.

Allan J. Hurst
President
Quorum Ltd.

[Hurst is a speaker best known for the educational programs he developed for sales, marketing, and management. He meets with more than 100 groups annually and has received awards from many trade and professional groups.]

All great companies have
been built by individuals.

Rupert Murdoch
Chairman
News Corporation

[Murdoch's News Corporation includes 20th Century Fox, the Fox TV and
FX Cable Networks, the *New York Post, New York Magazine,* HarperCollins,
a third of Britain's newspapers and half of Australia's, a TV satellite
network in Europe and Asia, and MCI.]

*The people who get into trouble . . .
are those who carry around
the anchor of the past.*

John F. Welch Jr.
C.E.O.
General Electric

[After receiving a Ph.D. in chemical engineering, Welch began his career with General Electric. He worked his way up to become chairman of a company currently enjoying its greatest success.]

P*ersistence propels potential to perfection.*

Soichiro Honda

Founder
Honda Motor Company

[Honda began in the motorcycle business and was an instant success. Despite the high failure rate in the auto industry, he successfully entered it and buried others in his way.]

You have no greater
leverage than the truth.

Good entrepreneurs are
risk-avoiders, not risk-takers.

Paul Hawken
Founder
Smith & Hawken Gardening Tool Co.

[After building Smith & Hawken from a mail order garden tool company into
a business generating millions in sales, Hawken founded a natural foods
company. He detailed his experience and knowledge in *Growing a Business*.]

If *[you] treat [your] employees correctly,
they'll treat the customers right.
And if customers are treated right,
they'll come back.*

J. W. Marriott Jr.
Chairman
Marriott Corporation

[Marriott is also a trustee for the National Geographic Society and a member of the national advisory board of the Boy Scouts of America.]

In order to get experience you have to get knocked around. . . . Experience, if it doesn't kill you, teaches you how to bounce back.

David J. Mahoney
Founder
Banyan Systems, Inc.

[After eleven years with Data General, Mahoney formed Banyan Systems to provide network operating systems to businesses. It commands almost half of the U.S. market.]

S*et your goals high and
don't let anybody tell you no.*

Muriel Siebert

President
Muriel Siebert and Company

[Siebert, the first woman to hold a seat on the New York Stock Exchange, became the superintendent of banks for New York State in 1977. The governor of New York later appointed her to regulate all of the state's banks.]

111

The way people deal with things
that go wrong is an indicator of
how they deal with change.

Rely on your intuition.

William Gates III
Founder
Microsoft Corp.

[Gates founded Microsoft to write programs for early computers. When he secured a contract to create an operating system for IBM PCs, Microsoft became an overnight success. Gates is considered the youngest self-made billionaire in the world.]

K*eep it cheap; keep it simple;
focus your energy.*

Herb Kelleher
Chairman
Southwest Airlines

[Kelleher uses his knowledge of military strategies in his business dealings. He credits his social and economic equality views to summers spent working on the factory floor of the Campbell Soup Company, managed by his father.]

Never underestimate a hungry, purposeful, committed company.

Eckhard Pfeiffer

C.E.O.
Compaq

[Pfeiffer took command of Compaq during a crisis. As a result of economic measures reached with employees, dealers, and suppliers, and by opening twenty-four-hour mail order and customer service phone lines, Compaq became the world's top PC vendor in 1994.]

Serve the customer.
Serve the customer.
Serve the customer.

Bernard Marcus

Cofounder and C.E.O.
Home Depot

[Marcus is a former president of Odell, Inc. and vice president of Handy Dan Home Improvement. His entrepreneurial spirit drove him to cofound Home Depot, Inc. The firm enjoys success by utilizing Wal-Mart's strategy of low prices and high volume.]

Nothing so conclusively proves
a man's ability to lead others as what
he does from day to day to lead himself.

You have to have your heart in the
business and the business in your heart.

Thomas J. Watson Sr.
Former President
IBM

[Charles Flint hired Watson to work for the Computing-Tabulating-Recording Company (CTR), which later became International Business Machines (IBM). As a CTR employee, Watson bought shares in the company until he became the major shareholder.]

N*ever allow your sense of self to become associated with your sense of job. If your job vanishes, your self doesn't.*

Gordon Van Sauter

Former President
CBS News

[A one-time president of CBS News and CBS Sports and a former executive of Fox News, Van Sauter recently became president and general manager of KVIE, a PBS station in Sacramento, California.]

T*reat everyone by the same set of principles.*

Stephen Covey

Chairman
Covey Leadership Center

[As chairman of Covey Leadership Center and the Institute for Principle-Centered Leadership, a non-profit organization, Covey conducts seminars for top business leaders worldwide. He has an MBA from Harvard and a Ph.D. from Brigham Young University.]

E*very addition to true knowledge is an addition to human power.*

Horace Mann

Founder and First President
Antioch College

[During his tenure as Secretary of the Board of Education, Mann visited European schools to study educational conditions and methods. Upon his return, he advocated the abolition of corporal punishment, arousing public sentiment for school reform.]

Hard work is the best
investment a man can make.

The man who does not work for the love of
work is not likely to . . . find much fun in life.

Charles Schwab
Former President
Bethlehem Steel

[In Andrew Carnegie's steel mills, Schwab worked his way through
various high-level positions until he was named president of Carnegie
Steel. He bought Bethlehem Steel Company from Carnegie and expanded
the business during World War I.]

You *are your first product.*

Portia Isaacson

Founder
Future Computing, Inc.

[After working as a computer scientist and retailer, Isaacson founded Future Computing, a PC industry analysis firm. She later sold it to McGraw-Hill. She is currently chairman and C.E.O. of Intellisys, founded to commercialize an integrated home-control system.]

Mistakes *will be made, but . . . [these]*
are not so serious in the long run
as the mistakes management
makes if it is dictatorial.

William L. McKnight
Founder
3M

[Born on a South Dakota farm, McKnight's first business transaction was trading a short-legged milking stool for a bookkeeper's bench. He built a successful company by empowering and motivating workers long before such terms entered the corporate world.]

W*hen one door closes, another opens; but we often look so long and so regretfully upon the closed door that we do not see the one which has opened for us.*

Alexander Graham Bell

Inventor and Former President
National Geographic Society

[From the age of 18, Bell worked on transmitting speech electronically. In creating a multiple telegraph instrument, he came up with the idea of a telephone, which he introduced at the Philadelphia Centennial Exposition in 1876.]

Support is "teamwork plus."

*You build a business
one customer at a time.*

R. David Thomas
Founder and Senior Chairman
Wendy's International

[In addition to founding and building Wendy's into a billion-dollar company, Thomas is the author of *Well Done,* a book detailing his life and the lives of other successful business leaders who built their businesses on strong moral principles.]

To *achieve your dream,*
you've got to dream about work.

Patricia Gallup
Cofounder
PC Connection

[Gallup and her partner, David Hall, founded PC Connection in 1982 with $8,000. David is the computer engineer, and Patricia is the business manager. PC Connection is currently the nation's largest mail order and catalogue PC and peripherals company.]

Motivate *[your people], train them, care about them, and make winners out of them.*

J. W. (Bill) Marriott Jr.
Chairman
Marriott Corporation

[In the 1980s, when his hotel empire was ridden with debt and failing, Marriott stepped in and reorganized the entire corporation. Marriott is once again a profitable corporation earning millions in revenue.]

I*f a man goes into business*
with only the idea of making money,
the chances are he won't.

Joyce Clyde Hall
Founder
Hallmark Cards, Inc.

[After founding Hallmark with her two brothers, Hall used her gifts as an innovative merchandiser, advertiser, and consumer researcher to make Hallmark synonymous with quality and style in greeting cards.]

G*rowth is a by-product of the pursuit of excellence.*

Devote 100 percent of your time to the critical issue.

Robert Townsend

Former President
Avis

[A former director of American Express, Townsend engineered a major turnaround that brought Avis into the black for the first time in 13 years. He currently works as an author and renowned speaker.]

$$\text{T}o\ get\ rich\ today,$$
$$you\ must\ help\ others\ get\ rich.$$

George Perrin
Founder and Chairman
Page Net

[After college graduation, Perrin took a job with the nascent Electronic Paging Trade Association in Washington, D.C. In 1981, he formed Page Net, which has become the largest paging network in the nation.]

S*tickability is*
95 percent of ability.

Dr. David J. Schwartz

President
Creative Educational Services, Inc.

[Schwartz, a professor at Georgia State University, is author of the national best-seller, *The Magic of Thinking Big*.]

*Learn to take risks and stretch
beyond what you think
your capabilities are.*

Ella Musolino

President
Sports Etcetera

[Musolino launched Sports Etcetera at a time when the U. S. Open had become the premier event in tennis yet remained underfunded. She began working with corporate sponsors and today handles billings in excess of $1 million for Merrill Lynch and other clients.]

Give me a stock clerk with a goal and I will give you a man who will make history. Give me a man without a goal and I will give you a stock clerk.

I will have no man work for me who has not the capacity to become a partner.

James Cash Penney
Founder
J. C. Penney

[Penney worked for several years at a Colorado dry goods store before he bought out the partners. At the time of his death, he had expanded Penney's to be the country's fifth largest merchandiser.]

Dare *to be different.*

Amelia Lobsenz

Chairman and C.E.O.
Lobsenz-Stevens, Inc.

[As a career public relations professional, Lobsenz was appointed by officers of the Rockefeller Brothers Fund to publicize their reports. Today, the Lobsenz-Stevens public relations firm has billings in excess of $4 million.]

There *is usually a fantastic opportunity if you are tuned in to hear its knock.*

Mary Jo Jacobi

*Corporate Vice President
Government and International Affairs*
Drexel Burnham Lambert, Inc.

[From a teaching fellowship at George Washington University, Jacobi became the number two lobbyist for 3M and then presidential liaison to the American business community. Later, she became corporate vice president for Drexel Burnham Lambert, Inc.]

I *have a lot of things
to prove to myself.
One is that I can live fearlessly.*

Oprah Winfrey
Harpo Productions

[Winfrey is the first black American woman to host a nationally syndicated talk show, for which she won an Emmy in 1987. She is also the first black American woman to purchase television and film production studios.]

Exhilaration of life can be found only with an upward look.

People come before product.
First things first.

Richard M. DeVos

Cofounder
Amway Corporation

[DeVos recently retired as president of one of the country's largest privately held companies. He is an acclaimed author and speaker.]

To be a manager, you have
to start at the bottom—
no exceptions.

Henry Block
C.E.O.
H&R Block

[Block started H&R Block with only his training in mathematics and bookkeeping. Initially, his only competition was taxpayers who filled out their own returns. Currently, H&R Block is a million-dollar company and the leader in its industry.]

F*eedback is the breakfast of champions.*

Kenneth Blanchard

Chairman
Blanchard Training & Development

[Blanchard founded his company to promote principles advocated in his books, seminars, and speeches. His client list is a "who's who" of corporations, associations, and institutions.]

T*he first step to achieving success is accepting the fact that nothing will ever replace hard work.*

Claire Gargalli

President
Equibank of Pittsburgh

[Gargalli began with Philadelphia's Fidelity Bank, becoming executive vice president and president. She moved to Equibank as senior executive vice president and was promoted to president. She is the highest ranking female officer of any U.S. bank.]

I*dentify . . . what you
want for yourself and
go for it.*

Masako Tani Boissonnault

Principal
ARCH-I-FORM, Inc.

[After graduation from schools in Japan and Los Angeles, Boissonnault
became a design consultant, working for several firms before starting her
own company. Her work has graced such clients as Diner's Club, TRW,
and Candle Corporation.]

Business is never easy,
but the difficulties are
not insurmountable.

Edgar S. Woolard Jr.
C.E.O.
Du Pont

[Since taking over the chemical giant, Woolard has tightened its bottom line and increased efficiencies. As a result, Du Pont has enjoyed significant success, and Woolard has won several prestigious awards for his efforts.]

*Success comes
from good judgment.
Good judgment comes
from experience.*

Arthur Jones
Founder
Nautilus Sports/Medical Industries

[Jones founded Nautilus in 1948 based on the variable-resistance
principles that revolutionized the fitness training industry.]

L*ove what you are doing and show it. Enthusiasm sells!*

Helen Boehm

Chairman
Edward Marshall Boehm, Inc.

[Boehm was one of the first women in New York licensed as a dispensing optician. After she and Edward married, they marketed Ed's porcelain sculptures. Today, Boehm is a world leader in fine porcelain.]

I'd rather have 1 percent of one hundred men's efforts than 100 percent of my own.

No one can possibly achieve any real and lasting success or get rich in business by being a conformist.

Jean Paul Getty
Founder
Getty Oil Co.

[Getty made his first million at age 23 in the Oklahoma oil business. He started the Getty Oil Company and in 1957 was considered the richest man in the world.]

The moment you let avoiding failure become your motivator, you're [already headed] down the path of inactivity.

Roberto Goizueta
C.E.O.
Coca-Cola

[Goizueta was a chemist at Coca-Cola's Havana plant when Fidel Castro took over Cuba. He moved his family to Miami and resumed his successful career.]

Credentials are not the same as accomplishments.

Robert Half

President
Robert Half International

[Robert Half International is the largest personnel service organization in the nation, specializing in providing personnel for accounting, finance, tax, banking, and data processing fields.]

I *feel every person can have everything if they are willing to work, work, work.*

Estee Lauder
Founder
Estee Lauder, Inc.

[Lauder started her career peddling skin creams her uncle produced. After one top-selling product provided a foothold, she built a billion-dollar cosmetics company.]

To control your tongue is
to control your very life.

*Experience a turning point.
Stay in the game – it's too soon to quit!*

William V. Crouch

President
Van Crouch Communications, Inc.

[Ranked as a consistent sales leader with American Express, Crouch
received many awards for outstanding performance in the insurance
industry and qualified as a member of the Million Dollar Round Table. He
is one of America's most versatile speakers.]

B*ite off more than you can chew, then chew it.*

Ella Williams

Founder and C.E.O.
Fletcher Asset Management

[Williams started her defense contracting firm with a small business administration loan, credit cards, and a second mortgage on her house. After winning an $8 million Naval Air Warfare Center contract, her work has won numerous prestigious awards.]

*Success . . . is simply
the natural outcome of our directed
intentions and actions.*

Ira Hayes
Manager
Advertising Department
NCR Corporation

[Hayes, a former president of the National Speakers' Association, is best known for his Positive Thinking Rallies.]

D*efeat is only*
a state of mind.

Dr. David J. Schwartz

President
Creative Educational Services, Inc.

[Schwartz's consulting firm, Creative Educational Services, specializes in leadership development. He is a renowned speaker and author, best known for his program, "Self-Direction for Personal Growth."]

Work is the meat of life,
pleasure the dessert.

*There is more credit and satisfaction in being
a first-rate truck driver than a tenth-rate executive.*

B. C. Forbes
Founder
Forbes Magazine

[Forbes started *Forbes Magazine* as a business publication that profiled leaders and discussed management policies and styles. His son, Malcolm, continued *Forbes* as a successful enterprise.]

F*ailure is not*
a fatal disease.

Earl G. Graves
Founder
Black Enterprises

[Graves, a political aide to Robert F. Kennedy, left politics to help involve the black community in business and government. Today, Black Enterprises is an influential voice for minority groups.]

Information is power, and the gain you get from empowering your associates more than offsets the risk of informing your competitors.

Sam Walton
Founder
Wal-Mart Stores

[After becoming one of America's richest men, Walton continued to drive a pickup truck, wear a Wal-Mart ball cap, and got his hair cut at the barber shop he had frequented for years.]

T*he path to success is to take massive, determined action.*

Anthony Robbins
Founder and Chairman
Robbins Research Institute, Inc.

[Robbins, a renowned speaker and best-selling author, consults with C.E.O.s, professional sports teams, and industrial leaders. His successful TV program is called "Personal Power," and he is the founder of nine different companies.]

The three great essentials to achieve
anything worthwhile are first, hard work;
second, stick-to-itiveness; third, common sense.

Everything comes to him who hustles while he waits.

Thomas A. Edison

Inventor and Founder
Edison Electric Light Company

[While working as a telegraph operator, Edison invented an instrument
that allowed messages to be transmitted over a second line without
operator assistance. He developed this into a machine that transmitted
numerous messages simultaneously on one line.]

The common denominator for success is work.

John D. Rockefeller Jr.
Former President
Standard Oil Company

[In addition to financing Rockefeller Center, Rockefeller contributed to Lincoln Center and helped restore colonial Williamsburg, Virginia. He also lobbied to locate the United Nations headquarters in the United States.]

About the Presenter

Van Crouch is widely regarded as one of the best and more versatile speakers in America. As the founder and president of the consulting firm, Van Crouch Communications, Van challenges individuals to achieve excellence in their lives.

After ranking as a consistent sales leader with the American Express Company, Van went on to receive many awards for outstanding performance in the insurance industry and has been a qualifying member of the Million Dollar Round Table.

Van Crouch authored the best-selling books, *Stay in the Game, Staying Power,* and *Winning 101.* Van is in demand for his thought-provoking seminars and keynote engagements to Fortune 500 companies, government organizations, church groups, and management and sales conventions worldwide.

Van Crouch has the ability to motivate people to raise their level of expectation. He is sure to both inspire and challenge you.

For more information about Van Crouch's seminars, speaking engagements, books, cassette tapes, and videos, contact:

Van Crouch Communications, Inc.
P. O. Box 320
Wheaton, IL 60189
TEL: 630/682-8300
FAX: 630/682-8305

Additional copies of this book are available
from your local bookstore.

If you have enjoyed this book, or if it has
impacted your life, we would like to hear from you.
Please contact us at:

Trade Life Books
Department E
P.O. Box 55388
Tulsa, Oklahoma 74155